HOW TO INFLUENCE PEOPLE AND MAKE FRIENDS

The Power Of Influence
In Friendship

By

Lincoln Greene

TABLE OF CONTENTS

INTRODUCTION........4
CHAPTER 1 6
CHAPTER 2 16
CONCLUSION..........22

INTRODUCTION

` Growing up as a kid, it has always been difficult for some group of persons or people to make new friends or to make friends at all unlike most people who have the power to influence a lot of much or as much as they want to.

This books pinpoints the reasons why most people find it hard to socialize and make friends and others don't. It also helps one understand the

concept of influence and how
it plays a big role in making
new friends.

CHAPTER 1

UNDERSTANDING THE REASONS BEHIND A KIDS/TEEN BEHAVIOR

Most parents feel weird or see their kids as weird and abnormal when they fail to make friends in school or even bring them home to hangout but they are unaware that the same way a kid strives and struggles to make good grades is equivalent to the way they struggle when making new friends.

Growing up as a kid, our parents have always educated us on the type of friends we make and keep but what they don't understand is that the world changes everyday, so what was easy to detect or see back in their days has become extremely difficult for us to identify.

Children (not all) would always want to obey their parents and keep to the word of their parents but when it comes down to making friends, they believe they have their own say or can have their own way, so they make friends with whoever they see fit. There are some set of children who are always anxious and stressed when it comes to making friends and its due to:

1. **They see themselves as inferior and others as superior:** In this case, children see themselves as not comparable to the others because they may not be wealthy like the rest or they feel most times they may not be able to follow the trend of what the others are doing so they tend to keep to themselves

and keep wishing that a miracle happens and end up not socializing with anyone due to that reason. When a kid feels this way, he or she can tend to do bad things like stealing in order to impress the other or gain their attention so they can get in their circle.

2. **They feel they need only their education:** Although this is quite good, that is focusing on your education in order to

make good grades, I consider it bad, why? Well, there is a popular saying that goes like "All Work And No Play Makes Jack A Dull Boy", meaning no matter how hard you think you need to work you also need to play. Also most friends help in studies because two heads are better than one, one person cannot know everything that's why there are different teachers for different subjects.

Also friends can be of big help to you in the nearest future so its advisable to make friends.

3. **Past Experiences:** Kids tend to keep a lot of grudges due to their young age. A kid must have put all his trust in one of his or her friends and got disappointed at the end which may have scarred them and the decided not to make any more friends in order to

avoid repetition of the same mistakes.

The only solution for all these is that parents increase their communication with their kids in order to know what trauma their kids have been through or to know a specific way to help the kid get back on his feet. Also kids need to be educated appropriately that most things are not meant to be therefore should not be forced or rushed because perfection

cannot be rushed.

CHAPTER 2

THE POWER OF INFLUENCE

People think making friends is the easiest thing to do in school because you are not the only one trying to make new friends and eventually someone would come and talk to you and you would both become friends but consider a school of over 200 kids and you probably transferred to a

new school where everybody
has made their friends and
probably not looking for any
more then what would you do?

Although it is possible that
some people may come to talk
to you to get to know you but
it all depends on you, are you
available or do you always
keep to yourself? All this
determines if you are going to
make friends.

According to definitions
from Oxford Languages,

Influence can be defined as the capacity to have an effect on the character, development, or behaviour of someone or something, or the effect itself.

Most people make friends based on certain principles; how they will be of importance to them, what class (wealth or status) they are in and even how they can be of influence to other people.

People tend to make friend with different attributes like

how funny they are, how
wealthy they are, how
influential they are and the list
goes on so when making
friends, one has to possess one
or more of these attributes.
Influence is the greatest
attribute because everyone
wants someone who can talk
and convince people and get
them on their side.

Being influential can not
only get you friends but can
also take you a long way in life

due to the fact that everyone who does not possess this attribute is looking for someone that does. Although it can get you a lot of enemies but who cares at least you have made friends like you wanted.

Being influential makes people want to be close to you because the way you speak and convince people matters a lot no matter where you may find yourself.

Having influence can help you by:

- Helping you develop strong relationships built on trust.

- Making it easier to achieve long-term goals.

- Improving your ability to lead an organization.

- Increasing your confidence and self-esteem.

- Garnering you public respect and praise.

CONCLUSION

Everyone has a boss as well as peers. To be successful, one must be able to work effectively with any or most of them. The lifeblood of this process is influence. In all likelihood, to be successful at your job, you must be able to "sell" an idea or project, persuade coworkers or peers to provide support and/or resources, or get people to do something that they may not necessarily want or need to do. The ability to move others to achieve important objectives is most effective if you can find a way to couch it in terms where everyone wins (you, me, and the organization). An underlying principle of persuasion is that people expect reciprocity in the process. To be able to persuade effectively, you must create win-win trades when in difficult situations or when dealing with difficult individuals or groups.